How to be a wizard

Important things that every wizard should know!

All wizards need their own broomstick – not just to fly, but also to keep their workshop tidy!

A cauldron for making potions is an essential piece of a wizard's kit.

All wizards have a trusty companion to help them make magic. Some have cats or frogs, but the most powerful wizards have owls!

A wizard is never without his own magic wand and spell book.

Potions have to be mixed with great care at all times. Make sure you are a responsible wizard!

Wizard club
Start a secret wizard club!

All wizards must keep in touch with what's happening in the wizard world. Start a club – it's the perfect way to share the latest potions and spells with your wizard friends!

Club Members

Wizard Fred
Wizard Jack
Wizard Lucy
Wizard Sarah

Only invite your closest wizard friends to join, and write a list with their names. Make sure that they're trustworthy wizards.

Club members could use a secret code to swap potion recipes and spells. The code below works by switching letters in the alphabet.

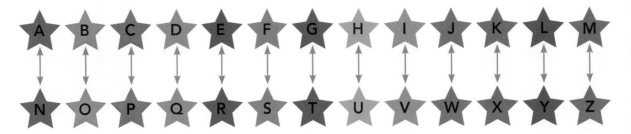

A	B	C	D	E	F	G	H	I	J	K	L	M
N	O	P	Q	R	S	T	U	V	W	X	Y	Z

Here's how to write "I love magic" using this code:

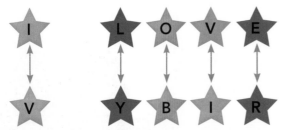

I — V   L O V E — Y B I R   M A G I C — Z N T V P

Wizard pictures

Copy or trace these fun wizard drawings

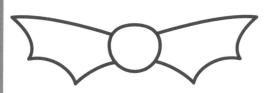

1 For a friendly bat, first draw a circle, then add a wing shape on either side.

2 Add ears, a smiley face and some detail to the wings. Finally, colour in your new bat friend!

1 For an owl, draw one large oval shape for the body, a maller oval for the head, then dd the eyes, wings and tummy.

2 Add ears, feet, a beak and detail to the eyes.

3 Finally, colour the owl brown, making his beak and feet orange. Use a lighter brown for the tummy and eyes.

1 For a frog, draw a circle with an oval inside, another val on top for the head, and vo circles on top of the head.

2 Add two arms as above, and then two legs to the side of the arms.

3 Colour the frog green, making the middle of his tummy a lighter green. Add detail to the feet, and a smile!

Magic potion

Make an explosive potion

You will need:

- 1 small plastic bottle
- bowl or cauldron
- vinegar
- baking soda
- tablespoon
- teaspoon
- food colouring
- liquid soap
- large plate or tray
- funnel

1 Using a funnel, fill the bottle until it is about one-third full of vinegar.

2 Add a few drops of food colouring. We have used green for this potion, but you could use any colour.

3 Add one tablespoon of liquid soap. Then put the bottle to one side.

4 Put the bowl (or cauldron if you have one) on a plate or tray. Measure three teaspoons of baking soda into it.

5 Pour the bottle mixture into the bowl or cauldron, and watch the magic take place!

Why not dress up as a wizard and make the potion in front of your friends to impress them?

Making magic potions always makes a mess, so remember to clean up afterwards!

Try experimenting with different coloured food colouring. Which colour makes the best potion?

Spell book cover

Make a magical cover for your spell book

You will need:
- book to cover
- coloured or patterned paper, about 5 cm bigger than the book on all sides
- coloured paper
- scissors • glue

1 Place the book in the centre of the paper. Fold the paper over to fit the top and bottom edges as above.

2 Place the closed book on the folded paper, 5 cm from one side. Fold the paper around one cover.

3 Remove the book and fold the paper crisply along the fold you have made. Slide the book cover into the fold and close.

You could make stars and stick them to the cover

My Big Book of Spells

4 When both covers are in their paper sleeves, shut the book. Now it is ready to decorate.

Why not add a spooky title to your book?

My Big Book of Spells

My Big Book of Spells

You could draw a picture to decorate the cover

Different materials such as felt make good decorations

My Big Book of Spells

Create a frame effect by sticking another layer of paper or felt onto the cover to decorate

Wizard hat

Make and decorate a fabulous wizard hat!

You will need:
- 2 large pieces of coloured card
- sticky tape
- pair of compasses
- pencil
- scissors
- coloured paper
- glue

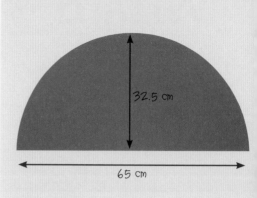

1 With the compasses, draw a large half circle on one piece of the card, about 65 cm wide. Cut this out.

32.5 cm

65 cm

Put sticky tape along the join

2 Fold the card into a cone that fits around your head. Stick the cone together with sticky tape, as shown above.

3 Place the cone onto the second piece of card as above. Draw around it to make a circle.

4 With the compasses, draw one circle bigger than the one already drawn, and one smaller circle, as above.

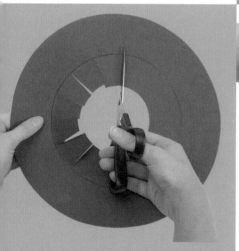

5 Cut around the largest circle. Then cut out the smallest circle, making a hole. Cut small flaps as shown above.

6 Turn the cone upside down, and stick the flaps to the inside of the cone with sticky tape.

You could decorate your hat with stickers

Why not make stars and moons from glitter paper?

Wizard wand

Grant wishes and make magic with your wand

You will need:

- star template (ask an adult to draw this onto card)
- 1 A4 sheet of blue card
- 1 A4 sheet of purple paper
- scissors • glue
- ruler • pencil
- double-sided sticky tape

1 Draw around the star template four times on the blue card. Then cut out the four stars.

2 Use the scissors and ruler to score a line down the centre of each star. Fold the stars in half along this line.

Glue here and stick to the back of this star

3 Stick the four stars together as above. Each half of each star should be glued to half of another star.

Stick double-sided sticky tape here

Keep wrapping until the pencil reaches the tape, then stick to secure

4 For the handle, stick tape as above. Wrap the other end of the paper around the pencil at a slight angle, to make a tube.

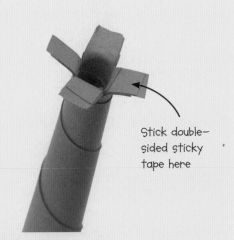

Stick double-sided sticky tape here

5 Cut four ½ cm long slits into the top of the thin end of the handle. Bend the flaps out and stick tape as above.

6 Line the four flaps of the handle in between the four spaces at the bottom of the star. Stick them to the star.

You could stick glitter paper to the star

Why not attach ribbons with little stars?

Wizard cut-outs

Cut out the wizards and friends and stick them onto card, or play with them as they are.

Wizard cut-outs

Cut out the wizards and friends and stick them onto card, or play with them as they are.

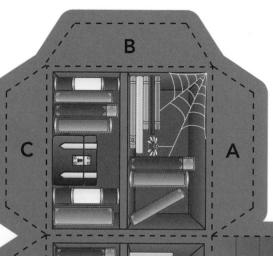

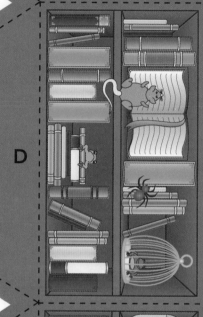

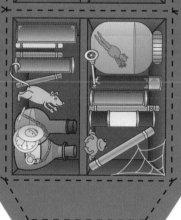

Wizard workshop

First, cut out the piece, then follow the instructions to make your wizard workshop. Why not create a wizard setting like this one?

Cut out Wizard Fred and play with him in the wizard workshop.

Tape tab A to the blue strip. Then tape tab B to the pink strip. Finish by taping tabs C to the purple strip and tab D to the green strip.

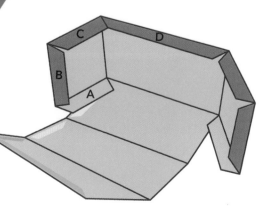

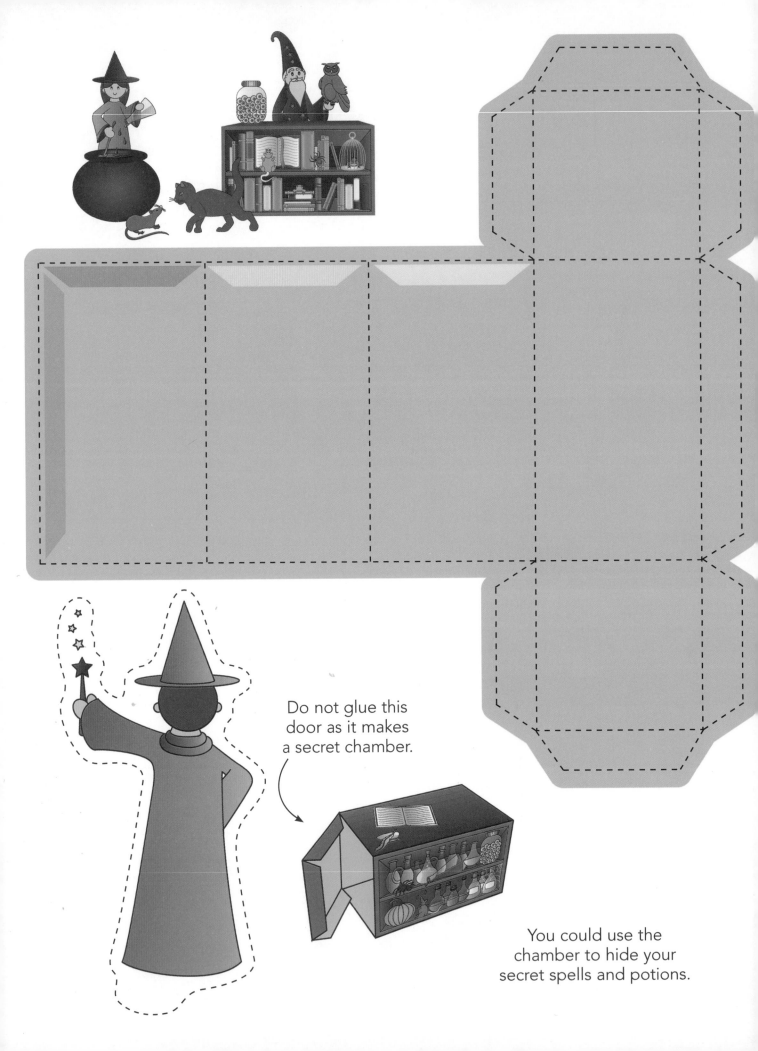

Do not glue this door as it makes a secret chamber.

You could use the chamber to hide your secret spells and potions.